The miracle of sex

self indulged pleasure and satisfaction

Bernard Scott, 2022

Table of content

Chapter 1

Sometimes a Miracle is Needed to Enjoy Sex

The majority of people believe miracles to be remarkable events. similar to the resurrection or the dividing of the sea.

A miracle is an uncommon and welcome occurrence that is not explicable by natural or scientific principles and is consequently ascribed to a divine intervention, according to Google's definition of a miracle.

The fact that you are even reading these words is very miraculous. It is very unlikely that you would have been born a human in this time period with any opportunity of finding this article. Nevertheless, here we are. a genuine miracle

Every small occurrence that occurs to us is filled with amazement, as we can see. We might choose to take things for granted or to consider them remarkable.

I like the philosophy of miracles that A Course In Miracles espouses. A miracle, in the words of ACIM and I paraphrase, is a change in perspective.

To see the reality of a situation, just change your perspective of it.

Chapter 2

A change in perspective.

We encounter a circumstance and have some opinions about it. If we have bad thoughts, we can label this circumstance a "trouble". We may also make the decision to look for a solution to the issue. Or, and here is where miracles occur, we discover the change in perspective to see that there was never an issue in the first place.

We have such a strong conviction that our ideas are accurate. that they possess a viable, subjective defense. However, everyone who has ever investigated this in-depth realizes that this is complete BS.

Instantaneous perceptual changes are possible. And when something like that occurs, it might seem very miraculous. However, it might potentially take years to develop gradually.

And sometimes it's a mix of the two: we expose ourselves to a range of concepts and methods, and then one day, apparently out of nowhere, KABOOM! Enlightenment. The issue is no longer present.

I know that miracles occur because of this.
In my life, I've seen a few miracles. These are the first two.

An example of a sudden, unanticipated miracle:

I was really unhappy for much of my adolescent years. I was lost in the sense that I didn't know why I was miserable all the time. I even considered it to be "cool." The pain of being alive...

I think I was depressed. Nothing made sense to me, but not in a suicidal manner. Nothing made sense at all. I was a wreck on the inside even though I seemed to be quite cheerful on the outside.

Then, one day, "out of the blue," I made the decision to alter that. to be content. to socialize. to be useful And with that, "miserable me" came to an end.

It was an impressionable time. And more than 20 years later, my new, post-resolution character is still in place An illustration of a delayed, sluggish miracle,It is the one that is always moving.

The wonder that is transforming me as it moves forward. You see, I already stopped enjoying my sex life about the age of 30. But over the last 12 years, I've evolved into a person who appreciates, celebrates, and seeks out greater sexual experiences.

Actually, my passion and purpose now revolve on sex. I want everyone on the earth to appreciate the wonder of healthy, meaningful romantic relationships.

I see a society in which having sex is accepted as a beautiful, natural, and sincere action. No guilt, humiliation, or embarrassment. And absolutely no coercion, wrong doing, or violence. These, in my opinion, are all products of a culture that views sex as forbidden.

This need not be seen as a miracle. It has been a never-ending transformational process. But I consider it to be a miracle. I mean, truly, from the first book I read that caused this transition to my serving as conference director for the Women's Sexuality Online conference last month. It tells the tale of the ugly duckling becoming a swan. I may choose to believe that this is a miracle. And I decide on magic.

Individuals may and do change,Some believe that persons are static. I must disagree, People are always evolving. Sometimes the change happens gradually, other times it happens quickly.

However, the change that really occurs may not be what you would expect to see.Non-linear and unexpected are both possible.But if we really want to, we can transform in a certain direction.

We need both effort and a miracle.What wonders do you want to happen?
Sometimes all it takes is a change of perspective to convert a searing agony in your life.All it takes is that. One epiphany.

In order to cope with a suffering in your life, there are also more intentional methods of changing your viewpoint. Personally, I like Byron Katie's "The Work." Examining your ideas and altering them to change your view is an incredible process that you can carry out on your own.

The moral of the story is to locate a miracle instead of waiting for one if you want things in your life to change.

Chapter 3

LOVE AND SEX

Although it is often a crucial component of romantic relationships, sexual intimacy is not always as important as one may assume. Both partners engage in sex for selfish reasons be it feels good and may increase self-esteem and for relationship focused reasons it deepens intimacy and appeases a partner.

Most relationships will eventually encounter sexual difficulties as people age and their desire for sex waxes and wanes (and generally declines). Research repeatedly demonstrates that most couples find it difficult to discuss sex openly, but that when they do, it makes them more compatible.

Although love might bring individuals together, it is not enough to keep them together. Many of us are familiar with relationships that failed despite having strong feelings for one another, whether it was due to one partner's adultery, their geographic separation, or other factors.

However, even in committed, long-lasting partnerships, lovers may drift away if one feels emotionally unsafe in the union or if there isn't enough passion or closeness.

Chapter 4

POWER OF SEXUALITY

Regular sex does assist to strengthen a couple's emotional link, according to study, but that benefit comes more from what it conveys than from the physical act openness, transparency, good communication, and a dedication to cultivate and sustain sensual energy.

After sex behavior is crucial as well The sensation of improved sexual pleasure after a sexual experience may make couples feel better about one other for weeks or even months, according to research on the sexual "afterglow," which includes hugging and pillow talk.

While many partners wonder why they may not have sex as often as they previously did or if they need to learn new methods, an improvement in a couple's sex life is more typically a reflection than a cause of other issues in the relationship.

The Influence of Love

A supporting connection is more likely to prevent death than giving up smoking or exercising, whereas a poisonous relationship is more harmful than having no relationships at all. Loving relationships may actually mean the difference between life and death.

The only way for love to last, however, is for both parties to be open and honest with one another, show their thanks, discuss their ideas and emotions, and seek for assistance rather than attempting to handle things on their own.

People sometimes think that by keeping their issues hidden from their partners, they are saving them, when they learn that the person they love the most has not confided in them or sought out their assistance, they may be very wounded.

Talking Sexual

Even relationships that are typically effective at resolving other difficulties have trouble discussing sex. People often believe that wonderful sex should not include talking, however this belief frequently results in years of boring or disappointing sessions.

According to research, people tend to avoid talking about uncomfortable subjects because they fear doing so will hurt their partner's feelings, especially if they discuss sexual fantasies or interest in "unconventional" sex, or because they don't want to reveal too much about themselves for fear of feeling ashamed or being shamed.

However, research also shows that partners who are open to discussing intimacy are generally happy in their relationships as they learn that their sexual problems are often not an indication that their relationship is in peril after all.

Chapter 5

SEXUAL ABUSE

Any sexual behavior that you do not consent to constitutes sexual abuse, including:

Inappropriate touching, oral, vaginal, or anal penetration, rape attempts, attempted rape, and child molestation

Sexual abuse may take the form of verbal, physical, or any other form that compels a victim to engage in unwanted sexual activity. Voyeurism (the act of seeing a private sexual act), exhibitionism (the act of exposing oneself in public), incest (the act of having sex with a family member), and sexual harassment are examples of this. It may occur by a stranger in a remote location, on a date, or at your house by a familiar person.

One frequent kind of sexual abuse is rape. It might happen on a date, by a friend or acquaintance, or when you believe you are alone yourself. Learn about the medications used for "date rape." When a victim isn't looking, they might be slipped into a drink.

No matter where you are, never let your drink get away from you. Always try to be conscious of your surroundings. Date rape medications impair one's ability to defend against attack and cause a kind of memory amnesia, leaving the victim unaware of what occurred.

Whether the abuser is a person you date, a current or former husband, boyfriend, or girlfriend, a family member, an acquaintance, or a stranger, violence against women is always unacceptable. It's not your fault. You are not to blame for the abuse that took place or for someone else's violent actions. Seek assistance from other family members, friends, or local groups if you or someone you know has experienced sexual assault. A sk for assistance or therapy. Consult a medical professional, particularly if you've been wounded physically. Learn how to decrease your risk of being a victim of sexual assault or sexual abuse before you find yourself in an uncomfortable or scary position.

Additionally, read on to discover how to receive assistance for sexual abuse and assault. Knowing whether you are in an abusive relationship is another crucial step in receiving treatment. If you are being mistreated, there are obvious indications that will let you know.

Chapter 6

WITCH OF SEX

Sexual energy is one of the most powerful energies that we can access since it's the energy that we're really generated from, and because sex is about what we intend, the intention that we make when we produce it,

The X element in witchcraft is sex. Serious practitioners and figures from witchy legend are both renowned for their capacity to awaken primordial cravings. In the instance of the medieval hags depicted in the 1486 witch-hunting book The Malleus Maleficarum, they even stole penises. Witches utilize sexual energy to converse, materialize, work magic, and take penises.

Sex magic has been a potent instrument in the hands of talented conjurers for millennia, but it has also been a discipline stigmatized by generations of terrified male historians. As a consequence, the complicated history of sex in witchcraft is a potent concoction of deceit, sin, and oppression.

Female sexuality was considered abominable during the early modern witch hunts in Europe (approximately 1300-1750), yet it was also a cultural fascination. It was believed that women's bodies and brains were more prone to vice and that they were thus more inclined to fall prey to Satan's seductive powers. In actuality, the stereotype of a witch riding a broomstick has an unexpectedly sexual roots.

Chapter 7

Sexuality and religion

Many individuals use sex for a variety of reasons. It seems to provide bodily gratification and release, but that's not all it gives. The emotional connection that sex fosters between lovers may increase closeness and trust. Some individuals even go one step farther and consider sex to be both a spiritual and a physical experience.

Like spirituality, there are several meanings of spiritual sex as well. Some individuals believe that spiritual sex is directly related to their religious practice. Others consider it to be a particular set of spiritual rituals also referred to as Tantric sex. Others, though, just regard it as a method of engaging in sex that results in a more profound, spiritually rewarding relationship with a partner.

Spiritual sex may be done in any manner. With such a wide range of interpretations, you can almost surely find a method to incorporate spirituality into your sexual life that seems natural to you.

Fallacies and Myths About Spiritual Sex

Contrary to popular belief, spiritual sex is not associated with any one faith. While certain types of spiritual sex may be related to particular religious traditions, anybody may engage in sex that they perceive to be spiritual.

Spiritual sex is supported in works by intellectuals from a broad range of faiths as not merely a possibility but also an essential component of one's own religious practice. Regardless of your own views, having spiritual sex is a choice; nonetheless, it is never compulsory. In fact, research suggests that those who self-identify as spiritual may engage in more regular sex

Chapter 8

THE PERCEPTION OF SEX

Although it has long been known that sex is one of the best ways to grab people's attention, relatively little is spoken about sexual preferences. Distinct religious and nonreligious ethical traditions have various views on sex, each of which is derived from a different set of underpinning assumptions about sexual interactions. Some people even think that discussing sex in public is wrong; if this is you, I suggest you to stop reading since I'm going to be fairly frank about this touchy topic.

A particularly tense debate between a conventional Christian perspective and what can be termed Liberal sexual views takes place in the United States on the issue of sexual beliefs.

In spite of the fact that the liberal perspective is, at most, a generalization of a few viewpoints, I will approach it as if it were a cohesive tradition. Of all, a lot of Christians have liberal views on sexuality, so these two groups shouldn't be considered as antagonistic so much as different. There are issues with both worldviews that merit discussion.

SEXUAL MYTH

Sexual myths are beliefs or assertions that people make about sexual topics but which lack any basis in fact, are exaggerated, or both. People's sexual health might suffer from sexual misconceptions on a variety of levels.

The impact of sexual myths on sexual health may vary based on a number of variables, including the degree of education of cultures and people, gender, age, the family, the surrounding social environment, and written and visual media. As a result of their connection to societal or sociological difficulties, certain sexual myths may not have an impact on a person's sexual life, but a significant portion of them may.

Individuals have different levels of belief in sexual myths. Depending on the region, different myths may have different rates of belief. In certain cultures, myths are commonly accepted. Similar to this, a person may reject certain myths as untrue or hold a variety of myths dear.
It might be crucial to choose the right response to sexual myths because of their variety and prevalence. The degree of belief in sexual myths has been measured using a variety of instruments [10–13].

Myths about sexuality might lower sexual pleasure. Sexual health and sexual functioning are also important factors in determining sexual satisfaction. To assess sexual health and function, certain scales have been created. The Female Sexual Function Index (FSFI) is a popular measure.

The Sexual Beliefs Scale and FSFI scales were used to measure the rates and levels of belief held by sexually active women, and the impacts of this circumstance on sexual functions and satisfaction levels, were also examined.

www.ingramcontent.com/pod-product-compliance
Lightning Source LLC
LaVergne TN
LVHW020545160826
845677LV00015B/4216

* 9 7 9 8 8 4 8 7 8 9 6 0 7 *